IMAGES
of Modern America

PAN AMERICAN
WORLD AIRWAYS

The US Postal Service issued a series of classic American aircraft stamps in 1997. The postcard shows the stamp commemorating the Boeing 314 Clipper, which was described as the epitome of luxury for air travel in the 1930s. (Author's collection.)

ON THE FRONT COVER: Clockwise from top left:
Pan American 747 jumbo jet (Author's collection; see page 53), Pan Am flight attendant (Author's collection; see page 37), Pam Am Worldport at JFK International Airport (Author's collection; see page 80), Pan Am Boeing 314 *Yankee Clipper* flying boat (Author's collection; see page 20), Pan Am Building in New York City (Author's collection; see page 83)

ON THE BACK COVER: From left to right:
Pan Am Air partner Omniflight helicopter services (Author's collection; see page 82), Pan Am Boeing 314 flying boat (Author's collection; see page 27), Pan Am Clipper passing the *Statue of Liberty* (Author's collection; see page 28)

IMAGES
of Modern America

PAN AMERICAN WORLD AIRWAYS

Laura J. Hoffman with retired
Pan Am captain Duyane A. Hoffman

ARCADIA
PUBLISHING

Published by Arcadia Publishing
Charleston, South Carolina

Printed in the United States of America

Library of Congress Control Number: 2014950332

For all general information, please contact Arcadia Publishing:
Telephone 843-853-2070
Fax 843-853-0044
E-mail sales@arcadiapublishing.com
For customer service and orders:
Toll-Free 1-888-313-2665

Visit us on the Internet at www.arcadiapublishing.com

This 1965 photograph of Pan Am captain Duyane "Dewey" Hoffman was taken in Plainfield, New Jersey. (Author's collection.)

CONTENTS

ACKNOWLEDGMENTS

This book would not have been possible without the support of my family and friends. Special thanks go to Nancy Hoffman and Mike Galloway for their support throughout this project, and to Linda and John Duffy, thank you for your patience. I also wish to thank my editors at Arcadia Publishing, especially Julia Simpson.

All images in this book are from the author's collection.

INTRODUCTION

I was a teenager when my father retired from Pan American World Airways (also known as Pan Am). As such, I did not have a clue what a major accomplishment that was, and it is only now—as I work on this project—that I begin to realize its significance. My mother, sister, and I were fortunate enough to accompany my father on his final trip—flying to Rome and spending several days there.

At the time, I thought it was pretty cool. We got to hang out in the first-class lounge, on the second level of the Boeing 747 jumbo jet, and I thought that spiral staircase was neat. I also remember not caring for the caviar that was served (not that I had ever tasted it before that day). There is one thing I will never forget, though: On the return flight, as we approached JFK International Airport, the copilot announced that this would be my father's final landing after 36 years of flying for Pan Am. After that one last, perfectly smooth landing, all of the passengers unbuckled their seat belts, stood up, and started clapping. Those passengers, complete strangers, showed their respect by giving my father a standing ovation. We were then ushered into the terminal, where Pan Am crew and staff staged a retirement party. It was 1978, and my father was 58 years old.

Oh, how the world has changed since then. Hijackers have become terrorists, and flying has become a nightmare. Few of us will ever have the chance to work for the same company for 36 years, and even fewer will be able to retire—by choice—at age 58. There are no more spiral staircases leading up to the luxury lounges of Clipper jumbo jets. Champagne and caviar are no longer served to passengers as they travel to exotic locations. There is no more Pan Am.

The history of Pan Am is conveyed quite well through postcards, thanks to the large number of them that Pan Am Corporate Communications issued through the years. The time frame for the company's existence also correlates well with the era in which postcards were a popular form of communication.

Pan Am founder Juan Trippe was a true pioneer in commercial aviation, putting the company on the leading edge with his innovation and determination. Born in 1899 in New Jersey, Juan Trippe became fascinated with aviation at an early age, after his father took him to an air show and race in New York City. Trippe was attending Yale University when the United States became involved in World War I, and he joined the Navy and was trained as a flight aviator. He returned to Yale after the war, graduated in 1921, and went to work on Wall Street. Continually captivated by aviation, he was able to channel his business acumen to become a business owner in 1922, when he purchased some ex-Navy training airplanes and started his first airline—Long Island Airways. That first venture did not last, but in 1925, after the United States government passed the Air Mail Act, Trippe founded Colonial Air Transport with a group of investors. He used his influence to bid on, and win, the New York-to-Boston airmail route, but after disagreeing with his partners on the best way to secure other routes, Trippe parted ways with Colonial Air Transport. In 1927, he used this experience to become involved in the merging of several airlines, which became Pan American Airways (PAA) and later Pan American World Airways. He successfully secured the first international airmail route from Key West, Florida, to Havana, Cuba, and on October 28, 1927, he put Pan Am on the map for the first time.

Juan Trippe first met Charles Lindbergh in 1926 at Teterboro Airfield in New Jersey—the year before Lindbergh made his legendary first-ever solo flight across the Atlantic Ocean on May 21, 1927. After Lindbergh became an international hero, Juan Trippe hired him to work for Pan Am in a technical consulting capacity—one of many forward-thinking decisions that elevated Pan Am's reputation as an elite airline.

In the mid-1920s, my father was growing up in New Jersey and liked to watch the airmail pilots fly overhead. In those days, airmail was delivered by the US Army, who navigated from town to town by following the railroad tracks. He told his grandmother that, someday, he wanted to fly airplanes. Less than two decades later, when the United States became involved in World War II, a critical need arose for more trained pilots, and my father got the chance to live his dream. In 1942, he was hired by Pan Am Air Ferries (a division of PAA), to transport aircraft overseas to support the war effort.

During his career, my father met Juan Trippe twice. The first time was in 1942, when he volunteered for a flight with a pilot who turned out to be Al Ueltschi—Juan Trippe's personal pilot. They flew from New York to Washington, DC, to pick up Trippe and return to New York. The second time was on June 28, 1959, when Trippe and his wife, Betty, were his passengers—returning home from a Bermuda vacation aboard a Pan Am DC-6 that my father was captaining.

Pan American Airways became Pan American World Airways in 1947. They were the first commercial airline to cross the Atlantic and the Pacific, the first to fly jets—and then jumbo jets—internationally, and the first to use computerized reservation systems. Pan Am was the exclusive airline of choice for people all around the globe, including Winston Churchill, the Beatles, and even Ian Fleming's superspy, James Bond. Juan Trippe was quoted as saying, "In the field of air transport, the true objective is to bring the life of an average man those things which once were the privilege of only a fortunate few." His pioneering spirit did that and much more. He retired from Pan Am in 1968 and died in 1981, but the world of commercial air travel evolved so quickly thanks to Juan Trippe and his legacy.

Pan Am's unfortunate demise in 1991 was caused by a number of factors, including an overly optimistic projection of passenger air travel, the high price of jet fuel, the over-inflated price paid to acquire domestic routes, and finally, the bombing of Pan Am Flight 103 in December 1988. As for my father, he has been retired now for 36 years, the same number of years that he flew for Pan Am. How many people get to live their dream for 36 years and then enjoy their retirement for 36 more? He is a true inspiration, and I am honored to be his daughter.

—Laura J. Hoffman

ONE FINAL NOTE: This book prominently features the art of John T. McCoy, who was a working student at the Curtiss Flying Service in 1926, where he met Charles Lindbergh. He was a pilot himself and served in the Army Air Corps in World War II. Pan Am commissioned McCoy to paint the First Flights series in late 1960s, and he consulted with Lindbergh on the selection of aircraft and locations for the series. He then circled the globe, visiting the various Pan Am sites upon which his paintings were based. His paintings were so authentic that Pan Am's public relations department used them on postcards and menus. All 13 of his watercolors from the series are featured in this book. He died in October 1993 at age 85.

One

THE BIRTH OF COMMERCIAL AVIATION

Commercial aviation took off in the United States after World War I. Barnstormers flew from town to town, delivering mail and selling rides and other services that included crop dusting, skywriting, aerial mapping, and even bootlegging. The Curtiss JN-4, fondly referred to as "Jenny," was very popular with many pilots. This original painting, by John Bachelor, was published by Dover in a postcard series called *Historic Airplanes*.

The Contract Air Mail Act of 1925 made it possible for private companies to bid on various airmail routes. Juan Trippe and company won Foreign Air Mail (FAM) Route 6 from Key West to Havana for Pan Am. This sign, marking the birthplace of Pan Am, hangs from Kelly's Caribbean Bar, Grill & Brewery on Whitehead Street in Key West.

Next, Juan Trippe initiated passenger service between Key West and Havana. John T. McCoy produced a series of paintings for Pan Am to commemorate famous first flights. This one shows the seven passengers boarding a Fokker F-7 bound for Havana, Cuba. This passenger flight was one of Pan Am's many aviation firsts. The 90-mile flight from Key West to Havana took place on January 16, 1928.

Key West is strategically located at the southernmost tip of the United States and is closer to Cuba than it is to Miami. In 1890, Key West had a population of over 18,000 and was the largest city in the state of Florida. The US government had begun the construction of two Martello towers in 1861. The east tower was built at the extreme northeastern edge of the island. In 1928, Pan Am built their landing field at this location.

The East Martello Tower in Key West was once a Civil War fort and later the site of Pan Am's first landing field. It is now the Martello Gallery-Key West Art and Historical Museum. It was added to the National Register of Historic Places in 1972, as it is the best preserved example of the Martello style of military architecture in the country. It is open to the public daily, except for Christmas Day.

In 1919, New York hotelier Raymond Orteig offered a $25,000 reward to the first aviator who could fly nonstop from New York City to Paris, or vice versa. Charles Lindbergh made history on May 21, 1927, when he flew across the Atlantic—from New York to Paris—in his single-seat, single-engine monoplane, the *Spirit of St. Louis*. He was a 25-year-old US Air Mail pilot when he won the Orteig Prize. Lindbergh's airplane can be seen at the Smithsonian Institution's National Air and Space Museum in Washington, DC.

This postcard reads, "Colonel Charles A. Lindbergh has requested the St. Louis Chamber of Commerce to reply to your congratulatory communication of recent date. The great volume of mail addressed to Colonel Lindbergh makes it physically impossible for him to personally reply to same. However, it is his desire that all his mail be acknowledged and that his thanks be extended to the thousands who have so generously felicitated him on his flight to Paris." It was sent from Harold M. Bixby, then president of the St. Louis Chamber of Commerce.

Juan Trippe knew the value of good publicity, and he hired Lindbergh as a consultant for Pan Am in 1928. Above is another John T. McCoy watercolor from the First Flights series. It shows the first airmail flight from Miami to the Panama Canal Zone—made on February 6, 1929, with Colonel Lindbergh in command. The 2,000-mile journey through seven Latin American countries took two and a half days. The Sikorsky S-38 amphibian was often referred to as "the Flying Duck."

Above is a first flight cover from the return trip of the same historic flight. It is postmarked February 9, 1929, in Panama and addressed to Juan Trippe in New York. On the back is the New York postmark from February 15, 1929. There was so much mail that a second companion airplane was used, and this cover is considered an "outlaw" because it traveled on the second plane and missed getting postmarked in Miami.

On September 15, 1928, the Pan American Airways Sea Terminal at Miami was opened, and all subsequent flights were flown from Miami rather than Key West. This John T. McCoy painting shows the first Pan American four-engine flying boat departing Dinner Key in Miami for Cristobal in the Panama Canal Zone for its inaugural flight on November 19, 1931. The route the Sikorsky S-40 took from Miami to Cristobal stopped in Cienfuegos, Cuba; Kingston, Jamaica; and Barranquilla, Colombia.

18:—"Off to Havana" on one of Pan American Airways Clipper Ships, Miami, Florida.

PHOTO BY G. W. ROMER.

The departure of planes was witnessed by large crowds who gathered daily to watch the flying boats depart from Dinner Key. The S-40 was the first aircraft to carry the Clipper name, which later became the call sign that identified Pan Am pilots to air traffic control.

PHOTO BY PAN-AMERICAN PHOTO SERVICE   8A-H1074

This is an aerial view of the International Pan American Airport showing the main terminal and hangar buildings. The roof of the terminal building had an observation deck and restaurant. Completed in 1934, this airport complex was one of the world's largest international airports and the main hub for air traffic between North and South America. Miami City Hall took over the terminal building in 1954, and it was added to the National Register of Historic Places on February 20, 1975.

M-26   HUGE GLOBE OF THE EARTH, PAN-AMERICAN AIRWAYS TERMINAL, MIAMI, FLA.

THE GLOBE IS 31½ FT. IN CIRCUMFERENCE AND WEIGHS 6,500 LBS.   PHOTO BY GERECKE

Inside the lobby of the terminal building at Dinner Key, Juan Trippe installed a giant globe that was 31.5 feet in circumference and weighed 6,500 pounds. The motorized globe was oriented so that its axis paralleled that of the Earth, with the North Pole pointed at the North Star. In the course of its rotation, the city of Miami comes to the top of the globe once every two minutes.

Here is another view of Juan Trippe's motorized globe, which resided in the lobby of the Pan American Airways terminal building at Dinner Key. This view gives a better idea of the size of the globe. It is now on display at the Museum of Science in Miami.

One of Pan Am's hangar buildings was used as an exhibition hall and auditorium for many years. It was renamed the Coconut Grove Convention Center and was the site of the March 1, 1969, incident in which Jim Morrison of The Doors was arrested for exposing himself to an audience during a concert. More recently, it housed the production of USA Network's television series *Burn Notice* from 2007 to 2013. The building was demolished in early 2014 to make way for a new 17-acre city park.

Two

Flying Boats

In June 1931, Juan Trippe wrote to six US aircraft manufacturers, asking them to design a flying boat with a cruising range of 2,500 miles that could accommodate a crew of four, plus 300 pounds of airmail. Only two of the manufacturers would consider the challenge: Sikorsky Aero Engineering Corporation in Bridgeport, Connecticut, and Baltimore's Glenn Martin Aviation Corporation. Trippe ordered three of each: the Sikorsky S-42 and Martin M-130. Above is John Batchelor's painting of the S-42.

This Pan American Airways S-42 flying Clipper ship linked the Americas with swift, regular schedules spanning the Caribbean Sea in a day. These four-motor flying boats weighed 40,000 pounds, and their cabins were wider than a Pullman car.

On August 18, 1934, Pan Am's *Brazilian Clipper* was the first Sikorsky S-42 flying boat to arrive in Rio de Janeiro. It carried 32 passengers at a cruising speed of 140 miles per hour and broke all distance records of the time. Shown here on an airline-issued postcard is a John T. McCoy watercolor of the S-42.

When used for passenger service, the S-42 held 32 passengers and five crew members. Its range was 1,200 miles, but on a survey flight, with more fuel and no passengers, the range was stretched to 3,000 miles. The S-42 was powered by four Pratt & Whitney Hornet engines.

The Sikorsky S-42 seaplane, originally named the *Brazilian Clipper*, was renamed the *Columbia Clipper* in the 1930s. Shown here leaving Dinner Key in Miami, this is one of the 10 S-42 seaplanes that were built exclusively for Pan Am.

© CLYDE SUNDERLAND 6A-H613

Pan Am had three Martin M-130 flying boats that handled the company's pacific routes. The *China Clipper*, shown here leaving San Francisco Bay on November 22, 1935, carried the United States' first load of transpacific airmail from San Francisco to Manila. In January 1945, the *China Clipper* was destroyed in a crash while attempting to land in the water near Port of Spain, Trinidad.

The *Philippine Clipper* arrived in Hong Kong on October 23, 1963, linking the United States and continental Asia by air for the first time. This McCoy watercolor shows the landing of the first flight, which carried 15 passengers at a speed of 130 miles per hour. The *Philippine Clipper*, which survived the Japanese attack on Wake Island in December 1941, crashed into a California mountain in foggy weather on January 21, 1943.

Each M-130 cost over $400,000, and Pan Am had three: the *China Clipper*, the *Philippine Clipper*, and the *Hawaii Clipper*. The *China Clipper* is shown here at Treasure Island in San Francisco Bay—Pan Am's western hub. Its sister ship, the *Hawaii Clipper*, made the first scheduled passenger flight to the Philippines. In July 1938, the *Hawaii Clipper*—with 15 passengers and crew aboard—mysteriously disappeared between Guam and Manila.

Pan Am's Clipper fleet operated on regular, weekly trips between California and the Orient. Stops were made at Hawaii, Midway, Wake Island, Guam, and the Philippines. These aircraft were capable of carrying a ton of mail, 40 seated passengers, or 18 sleeping passengers on a normal flight. With a fuel capacity good for 3,000 miles and a top speed of 180 miles per hour, they cut a month-long sea voyage down to five and a half days.

A cable station had been in operation on the Midway Islands since 1903, so there was some information available about the islands when Juan Trippe started to plan his airline's transpacific crossing. Two islands, Sand and Eastern, make up the Midway Islands, which are located 1,150 miles northwest of Hawaii. A coral ring surrounding the two islands creates a large lagoon that was perfect for landing seaplanes.

This "First Flight" envelope commemorates the journey across the Pacific that began on April 22, 1937, in San Francisco. From the postmark, the first stop was in Honolulu on April 23, from which point the plane continued to the Midway Islands, Wake Island, and Guam. The postmark on the back is from Manila on April 27, 1937.

Juan Trippe selected Wake Island, located in the Pacific about 1,150 miles west of the Midway Islands, as a seaplane base for its routes to the Far East. In 1935, Pan Am constructed a small village there called PAAville, which featured a terminal building and a hotel. In December 1941, only hours after the attack on Pearl Harbor, the Japanese attacked Wake Island. The Battle of Wake Island ended two weeks later with the surrender of the American forces.

Pan Am continued to use Wake Island as a scheduled stop on its route from the United States to China until the early 1970s. In 1971, the Japanese sent a workforce to dig up the remains of 786 Japanese soldiers. The remains were trucked to the ruined foundation of the old Pan Am Hotel, where they were cremated and the ashes flown home. There is not much left on Wake Island today except a runway what was used in May 2014, when a Delta Airlines flight needed to make an emergency landing there.

PAA (B314) Flight Deck Showing Crew   *LaGuardia Field*

Boeing came out with its version of the flying boat in 1939. The B-314 was the largest of the seaplanes and could carry up to 74 passengers. The flight deck of the B-314, seen here, was roomy enough for a cockpit crew of five, which included the pilot, copilot, navigator, flight engineer, and a radio operator.

PAA Yankee Clipper In Flight   *LaGuardia Field*

Here, the *Yankee Clipper* flies over LaGuardia Field in New York. The Marine Air Terminal (MAT) at LaGuardia Airport, known as North Beach, opened in 1940. Advertised as the world's largest airliner in service, the *Yankee Clipper* could carry 74 passengers and a crew of 11. It had four engines, a top speed of over 200 miles per hour, a 152-foot wingspan, and radio capabilities.

Pan Am's B-314 flying boat, the *Dixie Clipper*, completed the first transatlantic passenger flight from New York to Lisbon, via the Azores, on June 29, 1939. This John T. McCoy watercolor shows the B-314, which transported military personnel and supplies during World War II and carried many Allied leaders to important strategic missions on multiple continents.

Clipper leaving for Europe from Marine Terminal. La Guardia Airport

© PHOTO BY W. HOFF
OFFICIAL PHOTOGRAPHER
LA GUARDIA FIELD

63

The author's father mailed this postcard to his parents in July 1943. It shows the plane he was flying at the time, a Boeing B-314, as it left for Europe from the Marine Air Terminal at LaGuardia Airport in New York.

In 1939, five Boeing B-314s took over the Pacific flight routes. This postcard, which sent greetings from San Francisco, was postmarked in Ogden, Utah, on August 7, 1939, on its way to New York.

B-314s departed and arrived weekly from Treasure Island as a part of Pan Am's ever-evolving service—connecting 47 countries and colonies in 1939.

The six B-314s were christened as the *California Clipper*, the *Honolulu Clipper*, the *American Clipper*, the *Pacific Clipper*, the *Anzac Clipper*, and the *Dixie Clipper*. This postcard shows the *Honolulu Clipper* somewhere over the Pacific.

Considered the greatest of the flying boats, each of Pan Am's B-314s cost $550,000. When Pearl Harbor was bombed, a Boeing 314 was in New Zealand. With its Pacific bases attacked or abandoned, the seaplane was ordered to return via Australia, India, Arabia, Africa, South America, and the Caribbean. It arrived in New York on January 6, 1942, after the first (almost) round-the-world flight by a commercial airliner.

This 1939 painting by artist Gordon Grant, titled *The Yankee Clippers Sail Again*, shows the Boeing B-314. It was one of the most famous of the paintings commissioned by Pan Am.

Clipper passing Statue of Liberty   P A A Photo   80

Here, one of the flying Clipper ships passes by the *Statue of Liberty*. Pam Am's slogans included the following: "The System of the Flying Clippers" (1946–1953), "World's Most Experienced Airline" (1953–early 1970s), and "Experience makes the difference / Pan Am makes the going great" (early 1970s).

Three

LANDPLANES

Better airport facilities made propeller-driven aircraft more practical as they were less expensive to operate than the seaplanes. Pan Am acquired three Fairchild FC-71 high-wing monoplanes in 1930. Each plane held eight passengers and one crew member. With a 50-foot wingspan, the 35-foot-long plane had a maximum speed of 132 miles per hour.

On March 8, 1929, the Brownsville Municipal Airport opened and became the headquarters of Pan Am's Mexico Division. It had one of the first paved runways in the United States, and Pan Am mostly flew DC-3 and Convair aircraft into Guatemala, Panama, and Mexico from here. The facility closed in 1950. Capt. Duyane Hoffman was stationed here from 1947 to 1950.

229:-LINE UP OF PLANES, LA GUARDIA FIELD, NEW YORK MUNICIPAL AIRPORT

ADMINISTRATION BUILDING, NEW YORK MUNICIPAL AIRPORT, NORTH BEACH, NEW YORK CITY   46978

Pan Am ordered and received 16 of the DC-2 twin-engine aircraft between 1934 and 1941. Manufactured by Douglas Aircraft Company, most of these 14-seat passenger planes were flown into Central and South America, and Panagra (a joint venture between Pan Am and Grace Shipping Company) used many on their routes within South America. A former Pan Am DC-2 can be seen at the Museum of Flight in Seattle, Washington.

The Douglas DC-3, a fixed-wing propeller aircraft, was revolutionary in 1937, and many are still used today. It had a lasting impact on the airline industry and the military (where the model was designated C-47) in World War II. The DC-3 could carry between 21 and 32 passengers and two crew members. It had a maximum speed of 230 miles per hour and a cruising speed of 207.

Pan Am had a fleet of 90 DC-3s between 1937 and 1948. The DC-3 was responsible for making air travel popular in the United States.

The Lockheed Electra and Super Electra did not sell very well, as they held fewer passengers than the DC-3. Lockheed stretched the aircraft's fuselage by five and a half feet, allowing for two more rows of seats; thus, the Lodestar was born. The Alaska Division of Pan Am used Lockheed Model 18 Lodestars, which carried 18 passengers and three crew members.

A joint venture between Pan American World Airways and Grace Shipping Company led to the formation of Pan American–Grace Airways (Panagra) in 1929. Panagra operated primarily on the west coast of South America. In 1939, an American traveling to Buenos Aires would take a Pan Am S-42 flying boat from Miami to Panama, stay overnight, and then fly on a Panagra DC-2 or DC-3 to Buenos Aires, with overnight stops in Guayaquil and Santiago.

Created as a possible replacement for the DC-3, the Convair CV-240 was powered by two Pratt & Whitney R-2800 engines and carried 40 passengers. Pan Am had 20 of them between 1948 and 1957. This aircraft flew mostly in the West Indies, until Pan Am sold its Convair fleet in the late 1950s.

Pictured airborne over the coastline, the "Convairliner" was popular and had both civil and military variations. In 1960, John F. Kennedy used a CV-240 named *Caroline* during his presidential campaign—the first aircraft to be used in such a way.

The Boeing Model 307 Stratoliner was the first fully pressurized commercial aircraft, which enabled pilots to fly at 20,000 versus 10,000 feet for unpressurized planes. Not only did it allow the pilot to fly above bad weather, but it also provided a faster and smoother ride.

The four-engine, propeller-driven Douglas DC-4 saw use in World War II. After the war, DC-4s were introduced into the fleets of many commercial airlines, including Pan Am. The DC-4 could hold up to 86 passengers and four crew members. It had a top speed of 280 miles per hour.

Pan Am celebrated the inaugural flight of its commercial landplane service into the Belgian Congo with the arrival of a DC-4 on January 19, 1946, as shown in this John T. McCoy watercolor. This bimonthly service ferried passengers between New York and Leopoldville via Newfoundland, Lisbon, and Dakar.

The DC-4 marked the beginning of commercial airlines' transition to using landplanes for overseas flights. Seen here in flight over Miami in 1946, the DC-4 was the beginning of the end for Pan Am's world-famous flying boats.

This John T. McCoy watercolor depicts a leg of the first commercial round-the-world flight on June 29, 1947. The Lockheed Constellation *Clipper America* completed the global flight in 92 hours and 43 minutes, broken up over 12 days. The 20,000-mile trip featured landings in 10 countries and 17 cities. The Constellation, or "Connie," was a propeller-driven, four-engine aircraft known for its triple-tailed design and dolphin-shaped fuselage.

In September 1947, weekly round-the-world flights began to leave San Francisco. Flight 1—a DC-4—would depart on Thursdays, stopping in Honolulu, Midway, Wake, Guam, Manila, and Bangkok before arriving in Calcutta on Monday. There, it met Flight 2—a Constellation that had left New York on Friday. The planes would then switch flight numbers, and the DC-4 would return to San Francisco as Flight 2. The Constellation would leave Calcutta on Tuesday, stopping in Karachi, Istanbul, London, Shannon, and Gander before arriving in New York on Thursday.

The Boeing 377 Stratocruiser was a large long-range aircraft developed from the C-97 Stratofreighter military transport—which itself was derived from the B-29 Superfortress. It featured two passenger decks and a pressurized cabin. It was larger and faster than the DC-6 or the Lockheed Constellation.

Originally, flight attendants were called stewardesses, and airlines had strict hiring requirements. A stewardess had to be an unmarried woman of a certain age and weight. The age restriction was eliminated in 1970, and the restriction against hiring men went out in 1971, following the court case *Diaz v. Pan Am.* The no-marriage restriction was eliminated by the 1980s, and the weight restrictions were eliminated by the 1990s.

Frankfurt Airport was one of Pan Am's main hubs in Europe. The southern side of the airport grounds was home to Rhein-Main Air Base—a major air base for the United States from 1947 to 2005. When it was closed, the property was acquired by Fraport, the German transport company that operates the Frankfurt Airport.

This John T. McCoy painting commemorates the *Clipper America*, a Boeing B-377 that carried government officials and US Navy construction teams assigned to Operation Deep Freeze. The flight arrived at McMurdo Sound in Antarctica on October 15, 1957. This pioneering flight departed from Christchurch, New Zealand, and saw temperatures as low as 68 degrees below zero Fahrenheit.

Double-decker Clippers were the pride of Pan Am. Its distinctive fuselage and two decks for passengers set the B-377 apart. The long-range seating configuration provided seats for 75 passengers. Of these, 56 could be converted into Pullman-style berths, while the remaining passengers had sleeper seats. The lower deck served as a lounge and seated up to 14.

In January 1950, the Pan American Airways Corporation officially became Pan American World Airways, Inc. That same year, Pan Am ordered 45 Douglas DC-6Bs. The first was named *Clipper Liberty Bell*, which became the first to fly Pan Am's all-tourist class "Rainbow" service between New York and London on May 1, 1952.

The Douglas DC-6 is a piston-powered airliner that was originally built as a military transport near the end of World War II. It was reworked after the war to compete with the Lockheed Constellation in the long-range commercial transport market. Prior to 1962, it was known as the C-118 Liftmaster in the US Air Force and as the R6D in the US Navy. The *Clipper Midnight Sun* is shown here. The DC-6 had a wingspan of 117.5 feet and a capacity of 42 to 89 passengers.

This French postcard shows the distinctive tail of the Lockheed Constellation in the foreground, and a Douglas DC-6 in the background.

A total of 112 DC-7Bs were produced for Pan Am, starting in 1955. This one showcases Pan Am's postwar paint. The B series was considered the fastest of the Douglas prop-liners and was externally identical to the DC-7. It was the workhorse of Pan Am's New York to London route.

Shown here at Miami International in the late 1950s, the DC-7 CP was first introduced in 1953. It was the first commercial transport able to fly westward, against the wind, and still provide a nonstop cross-country flight.

The Douglas DC-7 was built from 1953 to 1958. It was the last major piston-engine-powered transport built before the jet airliner emerged in 1960. The DC-7C had improved long-range capabilities thanks to 3,400-horsepower R-3350 engines and increased fuel capacity in the longer

wings. A total of 121 were built, and Pan Am had 27 of them. Very few remain in operation today, due to engine issues. The Polar Route mentioned above refers to the great circle routes between Europe and the west coast of North America in the 1950s.

This envelope comes from the first airmail flight made on the Polar Route from San Francisco to Paris in the DC-7. The postmark on the front is from the departure in San Francisco on September 13, 1957. The back bears a postmark from Paris, dated September 14, 1957.

This postcard shows the DC-7 Steakhouse, which was located off I-75 in Byron, Georgia, about 90 miles south of Atlanta. This unique restaurant was originally a Panagra DC-7B, and the model was the largest propeller-driven liner owned by Pan Am. The fuselage was converted into a relaxed dining area. The restaurant closed in the late 1980s.

Four

THE JET AGE

Juan Trippe had the foresight to understand that the future of intercontinental air travel depended on the jet aircraft. Trippe signed orders for jets to be built by Boeing and Douglas on the same day in the 1950s, and the race was on. Boeing won the contest when they delivered the first jet to Pan Am. This postcard shows a Boeing 727 jetliner in the final stages of construction at the Boeing plant in Renton, Washington.

Boeing 367-80 (Dash Eighty)—

Roy Andersen

Collector Series®

© 1974 by Johns-Byrne Co., Chicago, Ill.

Boeing's prototype for the four-engine jet, the 367-80, was also known as the Dash Eighty. With the first flight of the Dash Eighty on July 15, 1954, the age of American jet transport began. It was used exclusively as a flying laboratory to test structural and aerodynamic advancements. Juan Trippe wanted it redesigned to make it longer and wider, with six seats across instead of five, and he wanted the wings to provide a third again as much lift and half again as much range. Boeing complied, and the 707 was born.

This John T. McCoy painting depicts the first jet passenger flight, which left from a rain-soaked New York International Airport on October 26, 1958. This was the first scheduled commercial jet flight by an American airline. The Boeing 707 carried 111 passengers to Paris in seven hours, reaching speeds of 575 miles per hour.

Pan American Jet Clipper

Pan Am was the first commercial airline to operate the Boeing 707. The inauguration took place on October 17, 1958, with a christening at National Airport that was attended by President Eisenhower. It was followed by a VIP flight from Baltimore to Paris. The Pan Am Jet Clipper began regular service on October 26, 1958.

The problem with the early Boeing 707s was an aerodynamic phenomenon known as the "Dutch roll." The airplane would not fly straight and was either nose left, right wing down or swinging abruptly back in the other direction. Boeing increased the height of the tail fin and added a vertical fin to alleviate the problem.

Panagra entered the jet age in the 1960s with a fleet of DC-8C Jet Clippers, only to merge with Braniff International Airways in 1967. Braniff operated the Panagra routes to South America until 1982, when Eastern Air Lines purchased its South American operations. Beginning in 1990, these routes were then operated by American Airlines, which had acquired them from Eastern.

To compete with Boeing, Douglas launched the DC-8 in 1959. Pan Am had a fleet of 19 of these four-engine, narrow-bodied long-range jets and used them for intercontinental routes. Capt. Duyane Hoffman flew the DC-8 for five years.

This preprinted postcard shows a Pan Am flight attendant and reads, "Hi—Welcome Aboard! Mr. Wood, President of Pan American Technical Schools, in West Palm Beach, Florida, has told me that you are interested in a career in the airlines. I am sure that Pan American Schools' Airline Career Program can help you realize your ambition as it has helped me. Who knows, we may even be working together someday. Good luck, Miss Muriel Wheeler."

In January 1970, Pan Am became the first carrier to put a 747 into service. The huge 747 offered passengers a cabin nine feet wider than the 707 (shown above), with a high ceiling all the way across so even passengers by the windows could stand up straight.

This John T. McCoy print shows the *Clipper Young America* arriving in London, marking the first commercial flight by the Boeing 747 wide-body jet on January 22, 1970. The crossing from New York to London took 6 hours and 43 minutes. The jumbo jet had a passenger capacity two and a half times that of the 707 and a crew of 20.

The Boeing 747 Superjet incorporated the most advanced technology of the day, including a fully automatic landing system and an Inertial Navigation System. Adapted from the Apollo Space Program, the INS would pinpoint the aircraft's position at all times without outside references.

A California man, Anthony Toth, has built a replica of a Pan Am B-747-200 inside a warehouse in Los Angeles. It tells the story of Pan Am Flight 120, from Los Angeles International (LAX) to London Heathrow (LHR) on a Boeing 747-200, the *Clipper Gem of the Ocean*. He got started by driving all over Southern California to visit aircraft bone yards, where retired planes are stored before being sold for scrap.

"Say hello to a brand new world." These red and blue seats were found in the forward first-class cabin. The "Clipper Class," which is similar to today's premium economy class, had light-blue seats and more legroom than coach, but not as much as first class.

This John T. McCoy painting shows the Pan Am *Clipper Constitution* as it arrives over Tokyo on April 25, 1976, having flown 5,478 miles nonstop from Los Angeles. The flight time for this inaugural, nonstop trip of the 747 Special Performance jetliner was 11 hours and 44 minutes. The 747SP was 47 feet shorter than a regular 747, and it had the longest range of any commercial aircraft.

The 747 was Juan Trippe's swan song, proving to be his last big innovation before retiring in 1968, but it became known as "Trippe's Folly" for several reasons. The price of jet fuel skyrocketed in the 1970s, which led to higher ticket prices. Jets flew with fewer and fewer passengers as a result. The 747 was expensive to operate, especially when it was only half full with passengers.

Boeing B-747-100-F   Roy Anderson

Collectors Series   © 1975 Johns-Byrne Company

The Boeing 747 was also used as a cargo aircraft, as shown in this watercolor print by Roy Anderson. Pan Am had three 747s that were used for cargo from the mid-1970s until 1983.

HONOLULU INTERNATIONAL AIRPORT

This postcard shows four different views of Honolulu International Airport, also known as the "Air Crossroads of the Pacific." The top left image is the Air Traffic Control tower, while a Pan Am 747 lands at Diamond Head in the top right. The colorful Wiki Wiki shuttle buses are shown in the bottom left square, with the airport's beautiful Japanese garden at bottom right.

The advanced 200 series of the Boeing 727 was introduced into regular service in 1981. Shown here, the 727 was meant to operate principally within the United States on short- and medium-length routes. The narrow-bodied 727 was the shortest of the Boeing jets, with the 100 series being 133 feet long and the 200 series being 153.

The Lockheed L-1011 made its inaugural flight on May 1, 1980. This John T. McCoy painting depicts the *Clipper National Eagle's* arrival at Simon Bolivar International Airport in Caracas, after a flight from New York. The L-1011 was the most fuel-efficient airliner of its time and held 18 first-class, 36 Clipper Class, and 190 economy passengers.

Pan Am had 12 Lockheed Tri-Star aircraft. In 1984, the Royal Air Force operated nine Tri-Stars—six ex-British Airways and three ex-Pan Am—that were acquired in the immediate aftermath of the Falklands War to bolster their long-range capabilities.

The Boeing 737 is a twin-jet, narrow-body airliner that is still in production today. Pan Am had 16 of the aircraft. The lengthened 200 series of the 737 first flew in 1968.

In May 1971, Boeing added more powerful engines and a greater fuel capacity to the 737-200s, which gave it a 15 percent increase in payload and range over the original run.

An Airbus A300 is shown at St. Thomas in the Virgin Islands in 1985. The A300 is a twin-engine, wide-body jet that could seat up to 266 passengers.

Airbus made a smaller derivative called the A310, which held 196 passengers. Pan Am used the A310 to fly select routes between Europe and the United States as well as Latin America and the United States in the late 1980s.

This postcard declares, "New ultra speed flying clippers for Pan American World Airways have been designed to make the world your neighborhood." Pan Am's public relations department continued to promote Juan Trippe's concept of making the world accessible to everyone. This "Preview of Tomorrow's Flying Clippers" displays a cross section of "private club comforts."

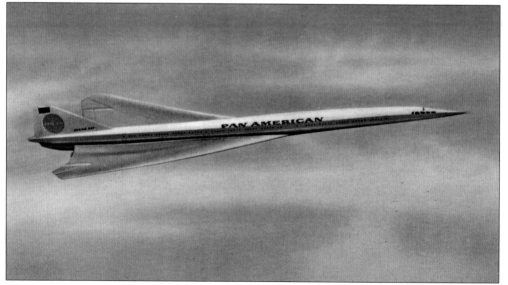

Pan Am was the first American airline to order the Supersonic Transport (SST) from Boeing. This airline-issued postcard claimed that the SST would fly from New York to London in 2 hours and 41 minutes. After Congress reversed its decision to provide Boeing with funding needed to develop the SST in 1971, none of the 15 aircraft ordered by Pan Am were delivered.

Five

DESTINATIONS

On October 28, 1927, pilot Cy Caldwell flew the first international airmail flight in a Fairchild FC-2 seaplane. The 90-mile flight from Key West to Havana was the first ever for Pan American Airways. In an airline-issued postcard series from the 1960s, every Pan Am destination was celebrated. This postcard shows Morro Castle, a fortress built in 1589 to protect the entrance to Havana Bay.

The US Post Office Department designated any airmail route flown by an airline to or from a foreign country as a Foreign Airmail (FAM) route. Bids were accepted for the various routes. On June 2, 1927, Juan Trippe and two others formed the Aviation Corporation of America. To win the bid for FAM-6 to Cuba, the airline merged with two others and formed Pan American Airways.

FAM-6 was awarded to Pan Am and inaugurated on January 9, 1929. It ran from Miami to Cuba, the Dominican Republic, Haiti, and finally, Puerto Rico. This airline-issued postcard touts the spectacular weather in San Juan, which averages 360 sunny days a year.

FAM-17 was awarded jointly to Pan Am and Imperial Airways. British-American reciprocal transatlantic service began on May 25, 1937, when the Imperial Airways flying boat *Cavalier* and a Pan Am Sikorsky S-42 left Bermuda and Port Washington, respectively, headed to the opposite airport. Pan Am began regular seaplane service from New York to Bermuda on June 18, 1937.

This airline-issued postcard shows a secluded cove on the island of Bermuda. It was not until 1948 that regularly scheduled commercial airline service by land-based aircraft began. The planes landed at Kindley Field, now known as L.F. Wade International Airport. Tourism in Bermuda peaked in the 1960s and 1970s, and now international business dominates the economy.

Arriving in Bermuda
Via Air

Compania Mexicana de Aviacion (CMA) became an affiliate of Pan Am when Juan Trippe took over the majority of their stock in 1929. FAM-8 was awarded to Pan Am, which operated the Mexican air service through CMA to comply with Mexican government regulations. A Ford Trimotor airplane, piloted by Charles Lindbergh, made the inaugural flight between Mexico City and Brownville, Texas, on March 9, 1929.

Another airline-issued postcard from Pan Am affiliate Compania Mexicana de Aviacion is shown above. CMA was Mexico's leading airline in the 1930s. Mariachis are shown playing in front of a DC-3. They flew Fairchild FC-2s and Fokker F-10s in the 1930s, and the expansion of their routes into the United States was made possible through their association with Pan Am.

This airline-issued postcard shows the Mayan pyramids of Chichen Itza, located on the northern part of the Yucatan Peninsula. It is one of the most visited archaeological sites in Mexico. In the 1930s, Pan Am started flying to Merida, the capital of the Mexican state of Yucatan and its largest city. The pyramids are about 100 miles from Merida.

Acapulco is one of Mexico's oldest coastal tourist destinations. It reached prominence in the 1950s as a place where millionaires and Hollywood stars would vacation, and Pan Am was the airline of choice to fly there.

FAM-8 was extended to Guatemala City—capital of the Central American country of Guatemala—on September 1, 1929. This postcard shows Guatemalan women carrying water in large earthen jugs perched on their heads. FAM-8 continued south to include Costa Rica, Honduras, Nicaragua, Panama, and the Panama Canal Zone.

This postcard shows an aerial view of King Cristophe's Citadel in northern Haiti. Built between 1805 and 1820 in the mountains overlooking Port-au-Prince, this massive stone fortress was intended to protect the newly independent nation of Haiti from French attacks. Pan American Clippers would fly directly to Port-au-Prince, the capital of Haiti.

An ancient Spanish cathedral wall in Old Panama forms the backdrop for a photo opportunity with a festively costumed beauty on this airline-issued postcard. When FAM-5 was combined with FAM-6, the route came to be known as the "Lindbergh Circle," with flights navigating the Caribbean Sea.

This airline-issued postcard shows the beach along Maracas Bay, near Port of Spain in Trinidad. While making a survey flight in 1929, Charles Lindbergh diverted from FAM-6 to land in Port of Spain.

On September 20, 1929, Lindbergh piloted a Pan Am Fokker F10A from Miami to San Juan, Puerto Rico. There, he and his crew switched to a Sikorsky S-38 to continue across the Caribbean to Paramaribo in Dutch Guiana (now known as Surinam). Lindbergh was accompanied on the flight by his wife, Anne, as well as Juan Trippe and his wife, Betty. The trip took three weeks and covered 9,000 miles.

This airline-issued postcard shows the world-famous Copacabana Beach at Rio de Janeiro, Brazil. The area was first serviced by NYRBA (the New York, Rio, Buenos Aires Line), but after a struggle, NYRBA was sold to Pan Am on August 19, 1930. FAM-10 went to auction the next day, and Pan Am won the route as the only bidder. Capt. Duyane Hoffman was stationed in Rio from 1946 to 1947.

This breathtaking view can be seen from a platform below the statue of Christ atop the Corcovado, a mountain in central Rio de Janeiro. Rio was an outstanding destination for Clipper passengers. Pan Am began flying there in the 1930s as a leg of FAM-10.

This Pan Am postcard depicts the lake region near Bariloche, in the province of Rio Negro, Argentina. The area emerged in the 1930s and 1940s as a major tourism center. It is situated in the foothills of the Andes, on the southern shore of Nahuel Huapi Lake.

FAM-18 was awarded to Pan Am, providing the company two routes east across the Atlantic to Europe. The southern route passed through Horta, Azores, and Lisbon, Portugal, on the way to Marseilles, France. The northern route went via Canada, Newfoundland, and Foynes, Ireland, on the way to Southampton, England. Here, a B-314 lands in the Azores.

"Pam Am makes the going great to Europe" is the slogan on the back of this airline-issued postcard depicting the beach at Estoril, near Lisbon, Portugal.

Shannon Free Airport and Industrial Estate, Co. Clare, Ireland. *Colour Photo by John Hinde, F.R.P.S.*

Unique in both its location and its place in aviation history, the Shannon Airport is the most western of all European airports. Located 15 miles west of Limerick in Central Ireland, it was the world's first duty-free industrial zone. Transatlantic aviation in the area began with a seaplane base at Foynes, but in October 1935, the Irish government decided to survey sites to find a base suitable for the operation of seaplanes and landplanes for transatlantic service. The result was the Shannon Free Airport, which opened in May 1939.

France has been a transatlantic destination since the early days of aviation. Pan Am's Southern Route was inaugurated on May 20, 1939, when Capt. Arthur E. LaPorte flew a Boeing 314 seaplane from New York to Marseilles. The Northern Route was inaugurated a month later, on June 24, 1939, as Harold Gray flew a Boeing 314 from New York to Southampton, England.

Alcazar Castle in Segovia, Spain, near Madrid, is shown in this airline-issued postcard. Spain was serviced by Pan Am Clippers through Barcelona.

A beautiful countryside near Oslo, Norway, is shown in this airline-issued postcard. Pan Am connected to a number of Scandinavian cities with regular flights.

With the old-world charm of its time-weathered buildings, Bruges was typical of the Europe that awaited Clipper passengers from all six continents.

This airline-issued postcard shows the island of San Giorgio Maggiore, at the entrance to the Grand Canal of Venice. Italy was serviced by Pan Am through Rome.

Heidelberg is located on the River Neckar in southwest Germany. Pan Am connected Germany with major cities throughout the world.

In Bavaria, the famed Castle Neuschwanstein overlooks Lake Alpsee. This region was serviced by Pan Am through Munich.

HAWAII, "Aloha State," 50th Star in OLD GLORY

This airline-issued postcard commemorates the 50th state with a first day of issue postmark from Honolulu. It reads, "The 50-star flag proudly presented here was announced as the new ensign of the United States on August 21, 1959 when Hawaii was officially proclaimed 50th state in the Union. The flag will become official on July 4, 1960."

Surfing is a favorite sport in Hawaii, and this scene at Waikiki Beach was a familiar sight to passengers on Pan Am's Flying Clippers. During the Vietnam War, Pan Am would transport American military service personnel on leave for rest and recreation to locations like Hong Kong, Tokyo, and Honolulu.

Starting in 1937, the harbor of Hong Kong was serviced by Clippers flying Pan Am's round-the-world routes. Hong Kong was included in FAM-14, which originated in San Francisco and flew across the Pacific Ocean to Manila in the Philippines.

Thailand's capital city of Bangkok was an important stop on Pan Am's round-the-world routes.

Fijian villages like this one were regularly visited by Pan Am Clippers en route between California, Hawaii, Australia, and New Zealand.

In the 1950s and 1960s, the Yesilkoy Airport in Istanbul, Turkey, had only one short runway. Opened in 1924, it is located on the European side of Istanbul, 15 miles west of the city. In 1980, the airport was renamed Anaturk International Airport. It now has three runways and is no longer the lone international airport in Istanbul. In 2013, it was the 10th-busiest airport in the world in terms of total international passenger traffic.

Over the years, fighting in Lebanon has changed the city of Beirut substantially. This airline-issued postcard shows the ancient Roman ruins of the Temple of Jupiter at Baalbek, 35 miles northeast of Beirut.

Another airline-issued postcard shows Jerusalem, with the Basilica of the Agony beside the Garden of Gethsemane. The Middle East was serviced regularly by Pan America's luxurious "President" and low-cost "Rainbow" flights.

Avalon Beach is a northern beachside suburb of Sydney, Australia, in the state of New South Wales. Pan Am began service to Sydney in 1947.

The current international terminal at Sydney Airport opened on May 3, 1970. The first Boeing 747 to arrive at the airport was Pan Am's *Clipper Flying Cloud*, on October 4, 1970.

FAM-19 was awarded to Pan Am, and on July 12, 1940, Pan Am flew a Boeing 314 from San Francisco to Honolulu, then to Auckland, New Zealand.

FAM-22 was the result of US military needs during World War II and was awarded to Pan Am. On December 6, 1941, one day before the bombing of Pearl Harbor, a Pan Am B-314 flew the first flight from Miami, via San Juan and Natal, Brazil, across the Atlantic to Bathurst, Gambia. From there, the plane went on to Leopoldville in the Belgian Congo. In the 1950s, Flying Clippers would serve the Union of South Africa regularly through Johannesburg.

Six

Odds and Ends

This Plane-Mate, from Budd, is similar to a mobile lounge or passenger transfer vehicle. This 1970s innovation eliminated long walks and other inconveniences at airports, allowing passengers to travel between their aircraft and the terminal building in comfort. These are used at the Dulles and Dorval airports.

San Francisco International Airport

San Francisco International Airport (SFO) was a major hub for Pan Am. Built in 1980, the international terminal at SFO includes an aviation library and museum. The San Francisco Airport Museum was accredited by the American Alliance of Museums in 1999. Some of John T. McCoy's aviation watercolors are on display there, courtesy of the Pan Am Historical Foundation.

The Pan Am Worldport opened in 1960 at John F. Kennedy International Airport. It handled thousands of passengers daily for many years. Delta Airlines acquired the lease on the Worldport in 1991, and it became known as Terminal 3. The terminal ceased operation and was demolished in 2013. The National Trust for Historic Preservation listed the site as one of 10 historic sites lost in 2013.

This aerial view shows the gardens and fountain at the International Arrival Terminal of John F. Kennedy International Airport in New York City. JFK is the busiest international airport in the United States.

This postcard shows the control tower and promenade ramp at JFK International Airport. Dedicated as New York International Airport in 1948, it was commonly called Idlewild Airport until 1963, when it was renamed to honor the memory of the fallen president.

Located at 200 Park Avenue and East Forty-fifth Street in Manhattan, the Pan Am Building was the largest commercial office structure in the world when it was constructed in 1963. Pan Am occupied 15 of the 59 floors. The building was sold to MetLife in 1981.

Omniflight operated Westland helicopters, like this one, for Pan Am at New York's East Sixtieth Street Heliport. Helicopter services were started in 1964 to assist New Yorkers with their commute to the airport.

A rooftop helipad offered service to JFK and Teterboro airports from 1965 to 1968. In 1966, travelers could check in at the Pan Am Building 40 minutes before their scheduled departure out of JFK. Helicopter service was suspended for good in 1977, when a Sikorsky S-61 toppled onto its side with the rotors still turning. One of the blades broke off and flew into a crowd, killing four people waiting to board the helicopter and one on the ground.

In 1964, an airline reservation management system was installed on the fourth floor of the Pan Am Building. That system, called PANAMAC, used the IBM 7080 data processing system and was designed by the military to provide real-time information to agents all around the world. Once again, Pan Am proved to be way ahead of its time.

K4SR
VIRGINIA

Amateur radio uses designated radio frequencies for private recreation and the noncommercial exchange of messages. Dated December 27, 1982, this QSL card from Virginia states, "This amateur radio operator is one of the proud thousands of present, retired, or former employees of Pan American Airways."

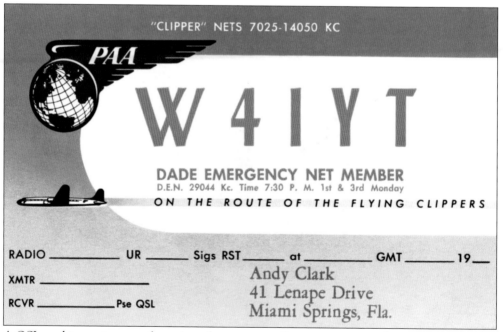

"CLIPPER" NETS 7025-14050 KC

PAA

W 4 I Y T

DADE EMERGENCY NET MEMBER
D.E.N. 29044 Kc. Time 7:30 P. M. 1st & 3rd Monday
ON THE ROUTE OF THE FLYING CLIPPERS

RADIO _____ UR _____ Sigs RST_____ at _____ GMT _____ 19 ___
XMTR _____
RCVR _____ Pse QSL

Andy Clark
41 Lenape Drive
Miami Springs, Fla.

A QSL card is a written confirmation of a two-way radio communication between two amateur radio stations. QSL cards are generally the same size as a standard postcard and are sent through the mail as confirmation of contact between stations.

QSL cards typically include the call sign of both stations that participated in the contact, the time and date of the contact, the radio frequency or band used, and other details of the transmission.

Collecting QSL cards was a hobby of some amateur radio operators, but fewer people physically mail the cards these days.

GRANDE HOTEL

no roteiro dos Clippers Voadores da *PAA*

BELÉM
Pará, BRASIL

Juan Trippe established the InterContinental Hotel brand name as a division of Pan Am Airways in 1946. The first of these hotels, the Hotel Grande, opened in Belem, Brazil, that same year. These accommodations were designed for Pan Am crews and passengers in locations where five-star hotels were not yet present. The hotel chain grew as Pan Am's routes expanded, first in South America and the Caribbean, then in Europe and Asia.

The InterContinental Hotel chain included the Piarco Guest House in Port of Spain, Trinidad, and the San Geronimo Guest House in San Juan, Puerto Rico. This airline-issued postcard was mailed to Long Island, New York, from Puerto Rico in 1951.

Piarco Guest House, Port of Spain, Trinidad

Hotel Grande, Belem, Pará, Brasil

San Geronimo Guest House, San Juan, Puerto Rico

PAA Guest Houses

The Hotel San Juan InterContinental was situated on a secluded 15-acre property that included 1,500 feet of private ocean beach.

Pago Pago is the territorial capital of American Samoa, located on the island of Tutuila in the Central Pacific. Its beautiful beaches and mountainous regions are a major draw for tourists. This postcard showing the poolside area at the Pago Pago Intercontinental Hotel was mailed in 1971.

After World War II, American Overseas Airlines (AOA) became the only commercial operator to maintain a full flight program during the Berlin Blockade. Pan Am acquired AOA from American Airlines in 1950. The Berlin Tempelhof Airport was located in south-central Berlin. It ceased operations in 2008.

From 1950 to 1990, Pan Am operated airline service between West Germany and West Berlin, first with DC-4s and DC-6s and later with the B-727. The Internal German Services (IGS) were launched as a result of an agreement between the United States, United Kingdom, France, and the Soviet Union at the end of World War II, which prohibited Germany from having its own airline.

Seven

THE END

In the 1970s, the Arab nations of OPEC declared an oil embargo, and the US economy found itself in the grips of an energy crisis. The price of all types of fuel skyrocketed, with the price of oil quadrupling in a year. The economy entered a recession, the public could not afford air travel, and Pan Am had a fleet of the biggest airplanes without enough paying passengers. This time, Pan Am missed the mark and misread the air travel market.

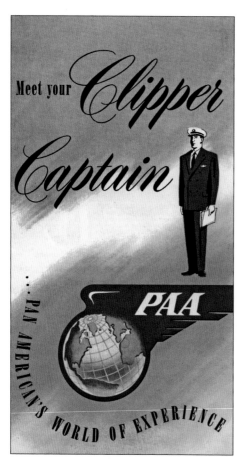

Meet your *Clipper Captain*

...PAN AMERICAN'S WORLD OF EXPERIENCE

PAA

The "World's Most Experienced Airline" continued to lack one crucial element—domestic routes. Juan Trippe sought to acquire domestic routes in every possible way, and during the 1950s and 1960s, Pan Am attempted to acquire various airlines, including American Airlines, Eastern Airlines, and Trans World Airlines. Trippe tried for years to influence the government to acquire routes, provide better airport landing fees between nations, and resolve discrepancies in finance fees.

Finally, Congress passed the Airline Deregulation Act in 1978. This allowed domestic carriers to begin flying internationally and was supposed to allow Pan Am to operate domestically. Despite the new law, Pan Am found itself shut out of the domestic market and now had to contend with more competition internationally.

In 1978, in a desperate attempt to gain domestic routes, Pan Am proposed a merger with National Airlines. Two other companies—Texas Instruments and Eastern Airlines—entered the bidding war and drove up the price of National's stock. After two long years of government delay, Pan Am was authorized to purchase National and, with it, got far more than they had bargained for.

Through the merger, Pan Am acquired National's fleet of 11 DC-10-10s and five DC-10-30s. Pan Am had paid over $400 million for National Airlines and, in return, received a host of problems. Two very diverse sets of employees had to be merged into one with a single pay scale and culture. In addition, Pan Am now had two incompatible fleets of airplanes.

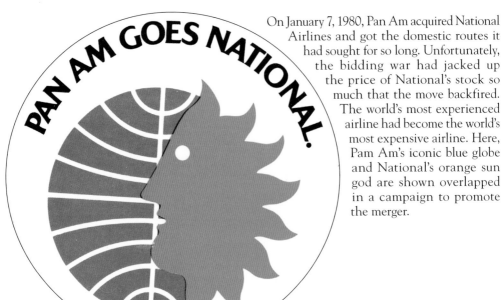

PAN AM GOES NATIONAL.

On January 7, 1980, Pan Am acquired National Airlines and got the domestic routes it had sought for so long. Unfortunately, the bidding war had jacked up the price of National's stock so much that the move backfired. The world's most experienced airline had become the world's most expensive airline. Here, Pam Am's iconic blue globe and National's orange sun god are shown overlapped in a campaign to promote the merger.

In 1981, Pan Am sold its pride and joy, the Pan Am Building, to MetLife—then a longtime tenant. Pan Am also sold the InterContinental Hotels Corporation (IHC) to Grand Metropolitan, a hotel company from the United Kingdom. It still was not enough.

In April 1985, Pan Am sold its Pacific Division to United Airlines for $750 million. As part of the deal, United acquired a fleet of 11 Special Performance Boeing 747s. The postcard above explains that the aircraft shown (N150UA) is the former N529PA of the Pan Am fleet—the *Clipper America*.

In 1986, Pan Am Flight 73 was hijacked while on the ground in Pakistan. Many were injured, and 20 passengers and crew members were killed. Then, on December 21, 1988, Pan Am Flight 103 from London to New York was bombed by terrorists while in flight over Lockerbie, Scotland, killing 270 people. With their financial situation deteriorating, Pan Am sold its IGS routes to and from Berlin to Lufthansa in 1989. The following year, Pan Am sold its very successful London routes to United Airlines and enacted workforce reductions.

The end was near as Pan Am's future flew off into the sunset. Despite making major cutbacks and selling off multiple assets, Pan Am was forced to declare bankruptcy on January 8, 1991. Delta bought their remaining European routes and the Pan Am Worldport at JFK International Airport. Reorganization efforts failed, and by November of the same year, it was all over.

In 1964, Pan Am started accepting reservations for future flights to the moon. Approximately 93,000 signed up for Pan Am's First Moon Flights Club, with an expected departure in the year 2000. Pan Am even had employees working with NASA at the Kennedy Space Center during the 1960s. This postcard shows an artist's concept of a Pan Am Ferry Rocket sitting on Pad 39A of the Kennedy Space Center. Unfortunately, Pan Am's rocket dreams never got off the ground.

BIBLIOGRAPHY

Banning, Gene. *Airlines of Pan American since 1927: Its Airlines, its People, and its Aircraft*. McLean, VA: Paladwr Press, 2001.

Daley, Robert. *An American Saga: Juan Trippe and His Pan Am Empire*. New York: Random House, 1980.

Gandt, Robert. *Skygods: The Fall of Pan Am*. New York: William Morrow Company, Inc., 1995.

Harris, Don. *Pan Am: A History of the Airline that Defined an Age*. San Bernardino, CA: Golgotha Press, 2011.

Heppenheimer, T.A. *Turbulent Skies: The History of Commercial Aviation*. New York: John Wiley & Sons, Inc., 1995.

Sutter, Joe. *747: Creating the World's First Jumbo Jet and Other Adventures from a Life in Aviation*. New York: HarperCollins Publishers, 2006.

DISCOVER THOUSANDS OF LOCAL HISTORY BOOKS FEATURING MILLIONS OF VINTAGE IMAGES

Arcadia Publishing, the leading local history publisher in the United States, is committed to making history accessible and meaningful through publishing books that celebrate and preserve the heritage of America's people and places.

Find more books like this at
www.arcadiapublishing.com

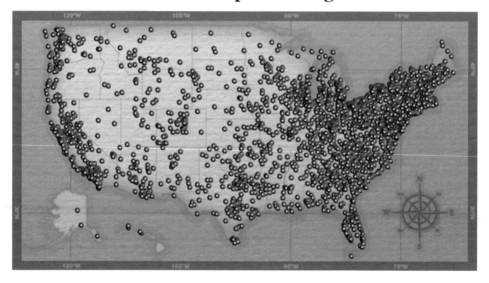

Search for your hometown history, your old stomping grounds, and even your favorite sports team.